Flying High

Program Consultants

Stephanie Abraham Hirsh, Ph.D.
Associate Director
National Staff Development Council
Dallas, Texas

Louise Matteoni, Ph.D.
Professor of Education
Brooklyn College
City University of New York

Karen Tindel Wiggins
Social Studies Consultant
Richardson Independent School District
Richardson, Texas

Renee Levitt
Educational Consultant
Scarsdale, New York

 **Steck-Vaughn Company**

A Subsidiary of National Education Corporation

MOMENTS IN AMERICAN HISTORY

Flying High

BY
Melissa Stone

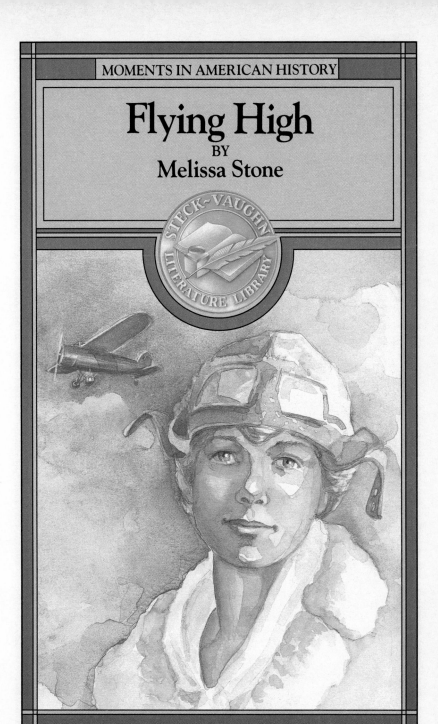

STECK-VAUGHN
LITERATURE LIBRARY

Steck-Vaughn Literature Library
Moments in American History

RISKING IT ALL
REBELLION'S SONG
CREATIVE DAYS
RACING TO THE WEST
YOU DON'T OWN ME!
CLOUDS OF WAR
A CRY FOR ACTION
LARGER THAN LIFE
FLYING HIGH
BRIGHTER TOMORROWS

Illustrations: Rae Ecklund: cover art, pp. 8-9, 11, 13, 14, 17, 19; Ron Himler: pp. 20-21, 23, 25, 26, 28, 31; D. J. Simison: pp. 32-33, 34, 37, 38, 41, 43; Al Fiorentino: pp. 44-45, 47, 48, 51, 53, 55; Brian Pinkney: pp. 56-57, 58, 61, 63, 64, 67; Frederick Porter: pp. 68-69, 70, 73, 75, 77, 79.

Project Editor: Anne Souby

Design: Kirchoff/Wohlberg, Inc.

ISBN 0-8114-4083-4 (pbk.)
ISBN 0-8114-2673-4 (lib. bdg.)   LC 89-110889

CONTENTS

1910

MARIAN ANDERSON ►
Her own homeland almost
refused to listen to her
remarkable voice.
(1908-1935)

BABE RUTH ►
His many home run hits
went straight to the hearts
of his fans.
(1902-1947)

◄ **DOROTHEA LANGE**
Her camera lens captured
the true picture of the Great
Depression.
(1912-1936)

1940

RICHARD BYRD ➤
This brave explorer faced
the dark Antarctic winter
entirely alone.
(1934)

➤ **AMELIA EARHART**
Her flight around the
world took her to an
unknown destination.
(1937)

AUDIE MURPHY ➤
His reason was simple:
why risk a platoon to do
what a single soldier
could handle?
(1942-1945)

AMELIA EARHART

PIONEER OF THE SKY

When I was a kid, my sister and I built a roller coaster in our back yard. I loved the excitement of coasting downhill with the wind and sky close to me! Today I fly high in the skies, and the winds coax my plane toward the stars. I love to fly! What great things I achieve! What greater things lie ahead?

I HAVE a feeling there is just about one more good flight left in my system." When Amelia Earhart spoke these words in 1937, she was already the most famous female flier in the world.

Photographs of her friendly, freckled face appeared in newspapers across the country as she broke one aviation record after another.

The public loved this tall, slender woman who reminded them of the girl next door. She was so full of life, so matter-of-fact, so unaffected by her fame.

"Find something you are good at and have fun doing it," Amelia advised her followers.

Amelia lived her life by this creed. She was good at flying. And to her, fun meant seeing the breathtaking beauty of the world from above, and challenging the unknown.

"You've done just about everything a person can do in a plane," exclaimed her friend and technical advisor, Paul Mantz. "You've flown solo across the Atlantic Ocean. You were the first person to fly over the Pacific Ocean from Hawaii to California. You've crisscrossed this country from coast to coast, setting speed and altitude records. What else is left for you to do?"

A smile flickered across Amelia's face. "I want to fly around the world," she said softly.

"Are you serious? All the way around the world?"

"That's right," said Amelia. "I want to do it at the earth's widest point — the equator."

No pilot, male or female, had ever attempted such a feat. That was one reason why Amelia Earhart liked the idea. She wanted to expand the limits of what was possible. She also wanted to show the world what a woman could do. But most of all, she wanted to do it for herself. She was never happier than when she was flying. This trip would be the high point of a lifetime.

Amelia, or AE as she preferred to be called, had dreamed of a round-the-world trip for years.

When Purdue University in Indiana set up a special aeronautical research fund in her honor, Amelia could finally make her dream come true. She purchased the well-outfitted plane that she would need for the flight.

"It's a twin-engine Electra! Isn't it beautiful!" AE raved to Paul, as she proudly showed him the new plane.

Paul nodded. But as he began fine-tuning the aircraft, he was filled with doubts.

"I'm worried about this trip, AE," he said. "Think of all the things that could go wrong — equipment failure, bad weather, faulty communications. You'll have to fly terribly long hours."

"I can handle it, Paul," she replied calmly. "I've made other difficult trips."

"I know, AE. But this will be such a long trip. At times you'll be out of radio contact with anyone. It's just too dangerous. Please, for your own sake, call off this flight!"

"Paul, this is a once-in-a-lifetime opportunity. Think of all the fascinating countries I'll see, and the sights — tropical jungles, vast deserts, snow-capped mountains! I'll meet people from all over the world! I'll experience things no one has ever experienced!"

"But, AE ..."

"Paul, I know what you're thinking. But what-ever happens, it will be worth it to me. You have to take a few risks in order to accomplish any-thing. I've always been happiest — most alive — when I was trying to achieve something."

"Well, AE, if anybody can pull this off, it will be you," Paul conceded.

O N May 21, 1937, Amelia and her navigator, Fred Noonan, climbed into the Electra. They left California and headed toward Miami, Florida, to begin their trip around the world.

As AE flew through the thin, wispy clouds toward Miami, her spirits were high. The joy of being airborne erased all doubts from her mind.

"At last!" she cried happily. "We're on our way at last!"

Upon reaching Miami, AE made one last survey of the plane. She discovered the special trailing antenna that Paul had installed.

"This antenna is too difficult to reel in and out while I'm flying. It's 250 feet long! I think we can do without it," Amelia said to Fred. She removed the antenna from the plane. "The radio should be enough. Besides, we need to make the plane as light as possible. This antenna weighs too much."

On June 1, Amelia and Fred took off from the Miami Municipal Airport to begin their flight

14

around the world. They flew to San Juan, Puerto Rico. From there they moved on to South America. Usually, they would spend a day or two at each stop. They would rest, sightsee, and greet the crowds who came to see them.

By June 8, they reached the west coast of Africa. From there they flew to Asia. Amelia visited a bazaar in Burma and sent her niece bright bracelets for her birthday. Next, they flew south to Australia, then finally to Lae, New Guinea. Amelia marveled at how much of the world she had seen in one month.

AT 10:00 A.M. on July 1, AE and Fred set out on the most dangerous leg of the journey. They had to fly more than 2,500 miles, then land on tiny Howland Island in the midst of the vast Pacific Ocean. The island was less than two miles long and only half a mile wide. If they missed it, they would find nothing but ocean for hundreds of miles around.

To help them locate the island, the Coast Guard ship *Itasca* was stationed nearby. Commander Warner K. Thompson and his crew stood ready to guide AE in.

"She's due at Howland at 6:30 tomorrow morning," Commander Thompson said. "At daybreak we will start sending up thick black smoke.

It should be visible for thirty miles. Bellarts and Galten, you're the best radio operators I have. I want you both to stay glued to your earphones for any message from her."

"Yes, sir," said the men.

A T 3:45 the next morning, Bellarts heard the first faint message from Amelia.

"*Itasca* from Earhart. *Itasca* from Earhart. Overcast. Will listen on the hour and on the half hour on 3105."

"It's them!" Bellarts announced excitedly.

He strained his ears for another message. At 4:55 A.M., she came in again. The message was unclear. The signal crackled with static, but it seemed a little stronger than the first one.

Bellarts felt his hopes rising. A stronger signal meant the plane was getting closer. Quickly he tapped out a return message in Morse code. He didn't realize how futile it was. No one on the *Itasca* knew that AE had left the trailing antenna back in Miami and could not receive the message. When his coded message got no answer, he tried a voice message. But he knew that on 3105 kilocycles, his voice would not carry far enough.

Bellarts and Galten waited silently, hoping to hear AE again. At last, at 6:15 A.M., another message came through.

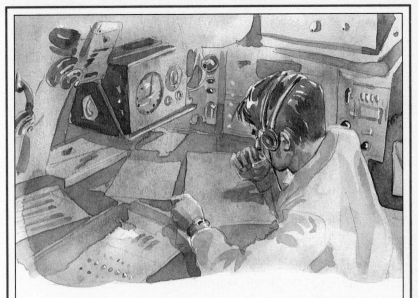

"Want bearings on 3105 kilocycles. Will whistle in microphone. Take a bearing on 3105 kilocycles." AE whistled into her microphone for a few seconds. "About 200 miles out," she said.

Bellarts and Galten tried to get a bearing on her. But she wasn't on the air long enough for them to pinpoint the source of the signal.

"We'll just have to wait for a longer message," said Bellarts with a sigh of disappointment.

At 6:45 AE's voice returned, again asking them to give her a bearing.

"About 100 miles out," she added.

Her voice disappeared long before the radio operators could locate her. Anxiously Bellarts sent a message asking her to use the emergency frequency.

"Please send on 500 kilocycles," he requested. But without her trailing antenna, Amelia could not use such a low frequency.

B Y now, everyone was worried. AE was officially overdue.

"She's been in the air over eighteen hours," Galten said tensely. "She should be here by now."

Time passed with agonizing slowness. Suddenly, at 7:42, her voice came booming over the radio. "We must be on you. Gas is running low. Unable to reach you by radio."

Bellarts and Galten looked at each other with alarm. Amelia sounded panicked. The signal was strong, but she couldn't be within 30 miles, or she would see the smoke signals.

Frantically the radio operators tried to establish contact with her. Bellarts began broadcasting nonstop, trying one radio frequency after another. Nothing worked.

At 7:58 A.M., AE called out again. "KHAQQ calling *Itasca*. We are circling. Cannot see island. Cannot hear you. Send signal on 7500."

Men up on deck scanned the horizon intently for signs of the Electra. Nothing.

At 8:45 A.M. another clear message came in. "We are on line of position 157-337. We are running north and south."

Then, as quickly as it appeared, Amelia's voice vanished. Only static filled the airwaves.

This last message indicated that AE didn't know her real position. She and Fred Noonan were probably flying back and forth in a north to south pattern. They could only hope to stumble across the island. For more than an hour, the men on board the *Itasca* tried to reach AE. With each passing minute, their spirits sank.

The *Itasca* immediately began a formal search. Soon other ships joined the rescue effort. They searched for days. Weeks passed, then months, then years. No trace of Amelia Earhart, Fred Noonan, or the Electra was ever found.

Even today, the disappearance of Amelia Earhart remains a great mystery. Yet, despite her tragic end, Amelia stands as a symbol of courage, determination, and high spirits.

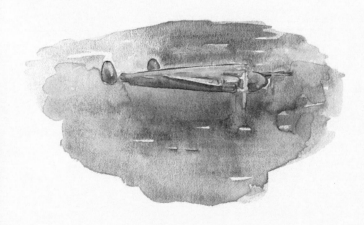

RICHARD BYRD

SURVIVOR OF THE
ANTARCTIC WINTER

Antarctica! It is the best place to study the earth's magnetism, cosmic rays, and meteors. And yet, for most of the year, it lies in total darkness. We know very little about this part of our planet. No one even knows how cold it gets. I must gather more information — I will spend the winter in Antarctica alone!

Y OU should be heading back to the permanent base at Little America. Your work here at Bolling Advance Weather Base is done," said Richard Byrd in 1934. He spoke to team members who had set up this base camp 120 miles south of the previously established coastal camp. "I'm disappointed that we didn't reach the South Pole and that we weren't able to transport enough supplies for two more people to stay here. But I'll be fine alone. One person can manage all the scientific instruments and collect the necessary data. You need to get back before the constant darkness of the Antarctic winter sets in. It's already March 28. The winter will begin soon."

"You have plenty of supplies, at least," said Pete Demas, the leader of the tractor transport. He surveyed the two long supply tunnels filled with food, books, and emergency provisions.

"I won't run out of anything," replied Byrd. He looked around the tiny wooden shack that would be his home for the Antarctic winter. "And it won't be hard to find things in here. When you've only got a space nine feet by thirteen feet to move around in, everything stays pretty handy. Thanks for getting all this ready! I know it was a hard job chiseling this pit out of eight feet of ice in temperatures of 50 degrees below zero."

"You're the one that will have the hard job — staying here alone all winter," said Demas. "Remember to make sure that the stove is venting properly. Otherwise, the fumes from the burning kerosene could be dangerous. Be sure to check that all the fumes are going outside."

"Don't worry," Byrd replied. "I'll check the venting pipes every couple of days to make sure they're working."

"I sure don't like to leave you here all alone." Demas shifted uncomfortably from foot to foot. "What if you get sick or injured?"

"I'll be fine," Byrd replied confidently. He had faith in his ability to handle any emergency. In fact, he was excited about the months that lay ahead. Then, locking eyes with Demas, Byrd gave one final order.

"No matter what happens, I'm giving a hard-and-fast order not to come for me until the winter is over. In a few weeks it will be dark 24 hours a day. Frigid temperatures, blizzards, and hidden crevasses will make travel treacherous. It will simply be too risky. Is that understood?"

Demas and the other crew members nodded somberly. One by one, they shook Byrd's hand. Then the group departed. Byrd watched until they faded into the horizon. He knew it was the last sign of life he would see for many months.

DURING his first few days alone, Byrd established a daily routine. In the morning, he took outside weather readings, ate breakfast, and did stretching exercises. Then he cleaned and adjusted all the weather instruments. After lunch came more measurements and observations, then a walk. Every Sunday, Tuesday, and Thursday he had lengthy radio conversations with the men back at Little America. He reported the weather data he had collected and took care of other business. In the evening he took a sponge bath, made more measurements, and cooked dinner. Then he played cards and read one of the books he had brought with him.

"It sounds like a calm, peaceful schedule," he thought. "But the reality is not that easy."

Indeed it was not. His oil stove died out every night, so the morning temperature of the shack was often 40 degrees below zero. Byrd had to climb into clothes that were frozen stiff. The kerosene he used to light his lantern was as thick as molasses from the cold. If he touched the frozen metal of the lamp, his skin stuck to it. He had to chop and melt ice for drinking water.

If he let his cup of water sit for a minute, it would freeze over before he could drink it.

Outside, temperatures ranged from about plus 10 degrees to minus 75 degrees Fahrenheit. Within days his nose, cheeks, chin, and fingers were frostbitten.

O N April 18, Byrd spent several hours outside, clearing a snowdrift away from the shack door. He noticed ice in the stovepipe. Although he didn't think much about it at the time, the ice was a sign that the ventilation system was not working properly. As snow blew into the

venting pipes, it melted. Then, when the stove died down, the melted snow froze solid. As ice built up in the pipes, fumes from the stove were forced back into the tiny shack. Although Byrd cleaned out the pipes every few days, that was not enough. The pipe seams inside the cabin were also leaking. Slowly, ever so slowly, he was being poisoned by carbon monoxide.

A couple of weeks later, Byrd experienced his first real problem from the fumes. At the end of the day he felt anxious and depressed.

"What is wrong with me?" he puzzled. "Why am I feeling so terrible?"

He could not think of a suitable reason. After all, his day had been quiet and productive. But as he sat writing in his journal, he felt a dull ache behind his eyes and a constant pounding in his head.

A thought crossed his mind. "Maybe the fumes from the stove are bothering me. I am certainly tired of the oily smell in the air." But, he concluded in his journal, "The most likely explanation is that the trouble lies with myself."

"Yes," he thought, laying down his journal, "I must be suffering from loneliness and depression. I can't allow myself to give in to solitude. I've got to be tough if I'm going to last all winter."

ALTHOUGH he didn't want to admit it, Byrd was becoming physically sick. Even when he was out in the open air, he felt weak and nauseated. Then, on May 31, after 70 days at Advance Base, Richard Byrd collapsed.

For hours he lay on the frozen floor of his shack. At last, however, a dim consciousness returned. He felt shooting pains in his head, his stomach, his eyes. He tried to move, but found that his hands and feet were numb. Through the haze in his mind, he realized that he had all the symptoms of carbon monoxide poisoning.

He managed to turn the stove off and crawl into

his sleeping bag. For the next three days he lay there, hovering near death. His body throbbed with pain. Although he was terribly thirsty, he was so weak that he could barely get out of bed and melt ice to drink. Every movement required excruciating effort. If the carbon monoxide poisoning did not kill him, the cold or starvation probably would.

Finally, on June 3, a thought floated to the surface of Byrd's hazy brain.

"Today is Sunday," he realized. "The crew at Little America will be trying to reach me on the radio."

Although he knew he was in trouble, he did not want anyone at the coastal base to find out.

"They might attempt a rescue mission," he thought. "And that I can't allow."

Byrd summoned his strength. He crawled out of his sleeping bag, cleaned the ice out of the stovepipe, reinstalled it, and lit the stove. As heat began to fill the shack, he made his way to the radio. There he struggled to send out a clear message. After signing off, he fell back onto his bunk, exhausted. The effort had sapped all his strength.

"I've got to stay alive," he whispered to himself. "If I stop sending messages, they'll know something is wrong, and they'll come for me!"

With every ounce of energy he had left, Byrd began his fight for survival. He remained incredibly weak. It required an iron will to force himself to do the basic things. He trained himself to move slowly and do just the most essential tasks. He kept the stove lit only during the coldest times so he wouldn't freeze. He took weather readings and sent them back to Little America. And he cooked meals even though he had to force himself to eat. It was a tremendous struggle.

Slowly, with agonizing sameness, June and July passed. Some days Byrd could barely make it out of bed. On his best days he only functioned at half-speed. He was living on nothing but his will power.

"I must last until spring!" he told himself again and again. "They must not come after me now."

BY late June the men at Little America were becoming suspicious. They noticed something was wrong with Byrd's radio messages.

"He always sends very short messages. And half the time they don't make any sense," the radio operator said.

"As soon as possible, I think we should head out to Advance Base," Demas declared.

The men all knew it wouldn't be safe until October. But they agreed Byrd might not make it that long. When the weather cleared for a few days in early August, Demas sent a message to Byrd saying he was on his way. Then on August 4, he and two others headed toward Advance Base on a snow tractor.

The trip was extremely harrowing. At one point they almost fell into a deep, hidden crevasse. But on August 11, 1934, they arrived at Advance Base.

Richard Byrd came out to meet them. He barely resembled the commander they had left four and a half months ago. He was scarecrow thin, and his eyes had sunk into his head. His hair was long and disheveled, and his clothes were dirty. He offered them some hot soup, then collapsed to the frozen ground.

For two months they took care of him and nursed him back to health. They were amazed that he had survived at all.

"I never knew a man could endure so long on sheer will power," Demas said softly.

DOROTHEA LANGE

PHOTOGRAPHER OF THE GREAT DEPRESSION

Photographs! Nothing is able to record an image with so much accuracy! Nothing else can reveal depth and details so precisely! My mind has always been my camera, clicking images and developing them in my thoughts. Somehow, I want photography to be part of my future. The eye of the camera sees so clearly. Maybe it will be part of what I give to the world.

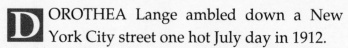

DOROTHEA Lange ambled down a New York City street one hot July day in 1912.

"I don't care what my family says," she resolved defiantly. "Somehow, someday, I *will* be a professional photographer! I just wish I knew where to begin."

Lange spent many days that summer trying to figure out how to make her dream come true. One day she walked past the shop of Arnold Genthe. Mr. Genthe was one of America's most famous photographers.

Lange saw her chance. Boldly she walked into the shop.

"Excuse me, sir," she said to the great artist, "I

would like to learn photography. Will you take me on as your apprentice?"

Looking at Lange, Mr. Genthe blinked hard. He couldn't believe this young girl had the nerve to ask him for a job. But he noticed a certain spark in her eye. It was a spark of determination, and of a desire to succeed.

"Yes," he said slowly. "Yes, I will teach you photography."

For the next few months, Lange learned everything she could from Mr. Genthe. At last she felt ready to take a paid job at another professional photography studio.

"Remember," Mr. Genthe told her as she packed her things, "when you first came here, you were nothing but a skinny, freckle-faced kid with a limp who didn't know a thing about photography."

Lange winced at this reference to her leg. She had had polio at age seven. It left her right leg shorter than her left, so she walked with a limp.

"But I looked beyond your appearance," Mr. Genthe continued. "I looked into your soul and saw something very special there. As you take photographs of people, you must always remember to look inside your subjects. That is where you will find beauty and truth."

Lange gave Mr. Genthe an affectionate hug and thanked him for all he had taught her. Over the next few years, Lange worked in many photography studios. She learned different techniques and gained experience with new equipment. But she never forgot what Arnold Genthe had told her. She always tried to look inside her subjects to discover what was underneath the surface.

IN 1918, at the age of 23, Lange moved to San Francisco. The next year, she set up her very own photography studio. Soon she had a reputation as an outstanding portrait photographer. Many wealthy people in San Francisco came to her studio to have their pictures taken. By 1929, she had a thriving business.

In the fall of that year, however, disaster struck. The stock market crashed, and the country tumbled into the worst economic depression it had ever experienced.

By 1932, the economy had hit rock bottom. A friend, Paul Taylor, huddled next to Lange over a cup of tea. "I just read in the newspaper that one out of every four workers has lost his or her job. A depression is certainly upon us."

"This is terrible!" Lange said. "What will happen to all the poor families and jobless workers? How will they manage?"

"I don't know," Taylor admitted. "Things look pretty grim."

That afternoon Lange stared out the window of her studio and saw a line of people.

"It's a bread line!" she murmured to herself. People were standing in line to get free bread. A rich lady in the city had set up the "White Angel Bread Line" to give food to the hungry. From blocks around, people came to wait in line.

As Lange looked at the people in the bread line, she saw outward signs of their condition — mismatched clothes, threadbare suits, downcast eyes, and bowed shoulders.

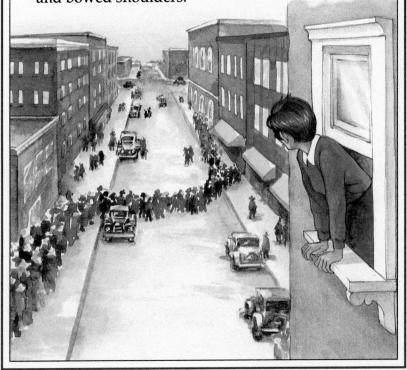

Then she remembered what Mr. Genthe had told her. When she looked in their eyes, she saw despair and hopelessness. An idea gripped her. She would capture what these people were feeling.

"I should be out there taking pictures of them," she realized.

Lange grabbed her camera and hurried down the stairs to the street. She looked through the camera lens at the people in the bread line. A blur of faces passed before her sight. Then she caught an angle that seemed perfect. She clicked the shutter and moved on to take more pictures.

"*This* is what I should be doing," she thought with a sudden sense of certainty. "From now on, I'm going to take pictures of real people in their real-life situations. No more posed portraits in a studio!"

AS the weeks went by, Lange spent more and more time out in the streets. She felt excited and challenged by this work, but she also felt scared. She was nervous about approaching people in their hour of misery.

"I don't want to invade your privacy," she explained to a group of longshoremen on the waterfront. "If you don't want me to take your picture, I won't. But I'm trying to capture what is happening in our country. I'm trying, with my pictures, to tell your story. Because it's not just your story — it's the story of millions of Americans. The Great Depression is affecting everyone — farmers, laborers, and business people."

"Go ahead," said the men. "Take all the pictures you wish."

That was the way most people reacted. There was something about Lange that made people respond favorably to her. Perhaps it was the sympathy and understanding they saw in her clear green eyes. Or perhaps it was the calm, soothing tone of her voice.

A T first, Lange exhibited her photographs only in local galleries. Her picture entitled *White Angel Bread Line* became a famous image of the Depression. It showed more than hungry people. It told the story of the Depression.

In 1935, the federal government hired Lange to document the plight of farm workers and other victims of the Depression. Each photograph illustrated the fears and hopelessness of the poor, hungry victims of the times.

In the spring of 1936, Lange found herself traveling in an old jalopy along the bumpy back roads of California. She went from farm to farm, photographing migrant workers. Many of them were farmers who had lost their farms because of the economy. These workers had no permanent home or job. They worked wherever there was a crop for them to pick. As crops ripened, these farm workers moved in to do the harvesting.

As Lange rounded a bend in the road one rainy afternoon, she saw a sign that read "PEA PICKERS CAMP."

"I wonder how these workers are faring," Lange thought, slowing the car. It didn't take long to find out as she walked through the camp.

"These people are desperate!" she murmured to herself. "They're practically starving!"

The pea crop had been ruined by a late frost. Since there was no crop to harvest, the pea pickers were not paid by local farmers. They had nothing to eat and no money to buy food. As Lange walked through the gloomy camp, she spotted one young mother and her children huddled in a makeshift tent.

"Hello," she said as she neared the woman, "I'm Dorothea Lange. I'm a photographer. I've been taking pictures of people in camps like this one. Would you mind telling me something about your life here?"

"Not much to tell," the woman replied sadly.

"I'm 32 years old. I've got five kids, but not a cent to my name. We've been living on vegetables that froze in the fields, but now everything's beginning to rot. In a day or two, we won't have anything to eat."

"Why haven't you left?" Lange probed gently. "Maybe there are other crops to pick farther south."

"We can't leave," the woman sighed. "I sold the tires off my car to get food for the children."

When the woman finished talking, Lange took some pictures. Then she thanked the woman.

"I will try to do something to help you," Lange said. "Who knows? Maybe my pictures will stir people into action. I certainly hope so."

As Lange walked back to her car, she felt a lump in her throat. Her heart ached for this poor woman, for her children, for the helplessness of all migrant workers during this Great Depression.

Back in her studio, Lange worked with a sense of urgency. She developed her pictures and hurried them to a San Francisco newspaper. The paper printed one of the pictures, along with a story about the 2,500 pea pickers.

The newsboys' shouts could be heard on each street corner. "Read about the starving migrant workers! Read all about it!"

As a result of the publicity, the federal government rushed 20,000 pounds of food to California to feed the migrant workers. And Lange's picture of the woman, called *Migrant Mother*, became the most famous photograph taken during the Great Depression.

THROUGHOUT the 1930's, as the Depression raged, Lange continued to take pictures. The faces in her pictures were bleak. They showed the enormous burden and hopelessness of poverty. They also showed the dignity of those who were suffering. But her photographs did more than just chronicle sadness. They helped stir action. They prodded the government to aid Depression victims — those who had lost their jobs, those who had lost their farms, and those who had lost their businesses. These photographs helped the public understand the problems of the poor. Because of Lange's work, millions of desperate Americans felt a glimmer of hope.

BABE RUTH
THE HOME RUN KING

Ladies and gentlemen, Babe Ruth is up at bat. Here comes the pitch. He swings. It's a hit! It's unbelievable! The ball is climbing! It's climbing! And now it's out of here! It's over the grandstand roof! Babe Ruth is running the bases now. The crowd is going wild! You can hear them in the next state! It's the first time anyone has ever hit a ball over the grandstand roof! Three times at bat! Three home runs! Babe Ruth — the greatest home run hitter ever!

HEY, George, let's play ball!" called the kids at St. Mary's Industrial School for Boys in Baltimore, Maryland.

Whenever he heard that, George Herman Ruth would run to take his place on the baseball field. He would drop whatever he was doing to play his favorite sport. He loved to throw a pitch and swing a bat more than anything else in the world.

Brother Matthias, athletic director of St. Mary's, often watched from the sidelines. He had been observing George since 1902. In ten years, he had seen him grow from a wild streetwise boy into an enthusiastic athlete. George seemed to have all the natural talent needed to develop into a skilled baseball player.

"I remember when George was first brought to us at St. Mary's," Brother Matthias remarked to Brother Michael. "He was only seven years old, but he had already been into more than his share of trouble. He spent all his time hanging around the Baltimore waterfront, in saloons and pool halls. He was a tough, foul-mouthed little kid."

Brother Michael raised his eyebrows. "Well, then, St. Mary's has had a positive effect on him. He has learned carpentry and cabinetmaking as well as becoming a talented baseball player. He is our star pitcher."

"I don't know how much credit St. Mary's can claim," said Brother Matthias, smiling, "but baseball has certainly had an effect on him."

Indeed, George Herman Ruth loved baseball. He loved the feel of the bat in his hands. He loved swinging at the pitch, hearing the crack of the ball on the wood, and watching the ball sail over the fence. As a pitcher, he also loved staring down batters. He'd grab the ball in his left hand, glower toward home plate, then wind up and fire the ball as hard as he could.

In the spring of 1913, a friend asked him, "What do you want to do when you leave here?"

"I can catch. I can pitch. I can hit the ball. I'll do anything a manager wants as long as I can play baseball," George answered.

Brother Matthias knew that George was a superb young athlete. He contacted Jack Dunn, owner and manager of the Baltimore Orioles, at that time a minor-league team.

"George Ruth is our star player. He lives and breathes baseball. He has the talent and drive to become a professional baseball player," Brother Matthias wrote to Dunn. "Please let him try out for a position on your team."

In 1914, Jack Dunn came to St. Mary's to watch George pitch. Dunn realized then that George had amazing athletic abilities. That very night he asked him to sign a contract with his Baltimore baseball team.

"I dreamed I would get to play professional ball, and now it has happened," George said to a friend. "This is it — my big break. And I'm going to make the most of it."

GEORGE reported for practice at Fayetteville, North Carolina, in the spring of 1914. He followed Jack Dunn all over the field, listening carefully for tips and instructions.

Another coach saw this and shook his head. "Here comes Jack with his newest babe," he said.

For some reason, the nickname stuck. From that day on, George became known as "Babe" Ruth.

George "Babe" Ruth did well with Jack Dunn's team. But within a few months Dunn ran into financial problems. He was forced to sell some players to other teams. The Boston Red Sox, a major-league team, bought Babe Ruth in July 1914 for $2,900.

Babe Ruth, only nineteen, pitched two winning games for the Sox in 1914, and won a regular position in the starting pitching rotation. He had a strong left hand and threw a great curve ball.

Over the next four years he piled up a record of 94 wins and only 46 losses.

Babe's pitching skills helped the Red Sox win the World Series in 1915, 1916, and 1918. By 1918, he was firmly established as a great pitcher and a Boston hero.

Babe Ruth hit his first major-league home run in the spring of 1915 against the New York Yankees. Over the next three years he hit a total of only nine homers. No one really cared — Babe was a strong pitcher, and pitchers aren't supposed to hit well. But Ed Barrow, manager of the Sox, recognized Babe's versatility and his ability to hit the ball. In 1918, Barrow made the bold decision to play Babe as an outfielder so he could develop as a hitter.

"A pitcher plays only once every four games," Barrow said. "But an outfielder plays every day. Let's see what Babe Ruth does when he gets more chances at bat."

Babe had no objections to this change. He liked to hit the ball and watch it sail out of reach. By the end of 1918, everyone was cheering the change. Babe hit .300 with 11 home runs. The next year he did even better, batting .322 and smashing in a record 29 home runs.

Boston fans went wild. They loved their Babe.

Everywhere he went, he was surrounded by mobs of people screaming for his autograph. He gave it cheerfully, smiling from ear to ear.

IN January 1920, Red Sox fans were already looking forward to another great season when they heard unexpected news.

"Extra! Extra! Read all about it!" Newsboys heralded the word from street corners. "The Red Sox have sold Babe Ruth to the New York Yankees for $125,000!"

No one could believe it. But it was true. Harry Frazee, the owner of the Red Sox, needed the money to invest in a musical play.

"I hate to leave my fans in Boston," thought Babe. "But baseball's what I love to do, and I'll play my best for any team I'm on."

For the next fifteen years, Babe Ruth played for the Yankees. He shocked the nation by hitting 54 home runs the first year he played with them. In 1927, he hit his all-time high of 60 home runs. During the course of his career, he helped the Yankees win seven pennants and five World Series. He became the most famous, and most loved, American sports hero of the time.

B ABE Ruth was an honest, kindhearted man who had a special love for children. He made countless appearances at hospitals to cheer sick children. Whenever Babe heard of a sick child who wanted to see him, he made it a point to visit. Perhaps his most famous visit was to a little boy named Johnny Sylvester.

On the day before the opening game of the 1926 World Series, Babe Ruth received a note from Johnny's father.

> I have a boy, ten years old, who just had an operation. The doctors say the surgery was successful, but Johnny seems to have lost the will to live. He doesn't respond to anyone. You are his greatest hero. Maybe if you sent him a letter or an autographed baseball, it would help him recover.

Babe did not hesitate. That very afternoon he appeared in Johnny's hospital room with an autographed ball, a glove, and a bat. He didn't notify reporters. He didn't want the visit to be a public spectacle. He just wanted to do what he could to lift the spirits of a sad, weak little boy.

When Johnny saw his idol walk into the room, his eyes brightened. He smiled as Babe sat down next to him on the bed.

"Now listen, Johnny," said Babe in his gentlest voice. "I'm going to make a deal with you. I want you to listen to your doctors and work real hard to get well. If you promise to do that, I'll make you a promise, too."

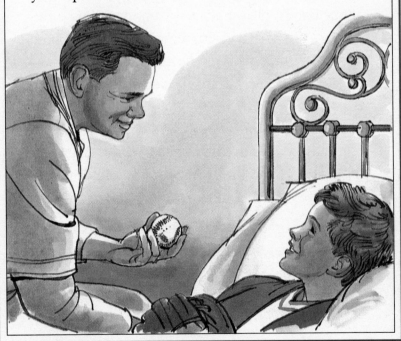

"What's that?" whispered the boy.

"I promise to hit a home run just for you. In fact, I'll do it tomorrow afternoon. Listen to the game on your radio. I'll hit one out of the park just for you."

Johnny promised to get well, then waved feebly as Babe walked out of the room. The next day, as Johnny listened to the game from his hospital bed, Babe Ruth belted a home run ball over the center field fence. For the first time since his operation, Johnny sat up. Tears streamed down his face as he cheered his hero. From that moment on, Johnny fought to get better.

Somehow newspaper reporters found out about Babe's visit, and it became headline news around the country. But Babe and Johnny both knew that the visit was no publicity stunt. Babe had come to see Johnny because he cared. Perhaps Babe's own lonely childhood had taught him the importance of caring. Or perhaps he just naturally could not resist a needy child. Whatever the reason, Babe Ruth changed the life of young Johnny Sylvester, and many others like him.

B Y the time Babe Ruth retired in 1935, he had the greatest baseball career ever known. He had won the hearts of millions of fans, both in America and overseas. He was photographed more than presidents, movie stars, and international leaders. People even referred to Yankee Stadium as "the house that Babe Ruth built."

Still, Babe's most important work may not have been done on the ball field. His biggest accomplishment may have been bringing hope back into the lives of kids like Johnny Sylvester.

In 1947, at the age of 52, Babe himself was very ill. His career was over. But Johnny Sylvester had not forsaken him. Johnny, now a healthy man of 30, heard of Babe's illness. He dropped everything and went rushing to see his old hero.

"I just wanted to pay him back for the visit he made to me," said Johnny. "I wanted him to know that I'll never forget him. He'll always be my number one hero."

MARIAN ANDERSON
A VOICE HEARD ONCE IN A CENTURY

Singing is everything to me. When I'm singing, I'm not concerned about anything else. And I love to share my singing with others. I try to connect with my audience. I want to bring them the beauty of the music and let them know the satisfaction of hearing more than just notes written on paper. My voice comes from my heart and my soul, not from the color of my skin.

NO one in the Union Baptist Church in South Philadelphia uttered a sound. The entire congregation sat, hushed, as six-year-old Marian Anderson stepped up to the front of the church. When the music began, Marian started to sing.

> He's got the whole world in his hands.
> He's got the whole wide world in his hands.

As the words flowed out of her mouth, people in the pews sat in awe. The child's voice was so beautiful, so perfect, that it gave new meaning to the familiar old tune she was singing. By the time

she finished, many people in the church were weeping with joy.

"Your daughter has great talent," said Alexander Robinson, the choirmaster, to Mrs. Anderson. "I certainly hope she can take voice lessons when she's older."

Mrs. Anderson nodded appreciatively. She, too, knew that her daughter had a special gift. But the year was 1908, and the Andersons were poor. What chance did they have of giving Marian the luxury of expensive music lessons?

As Marian grew older, music became the great love of her life. Somehow, when she was singing, all her troubles vanished and she felt completely free. Singing in the choir every Sunday became the highlight of her week. Many times Marian sang solos for the large congregation. Often the minister would comment on her beautiful voice.

But tragedy struck the Anderson household. Marian's father died. The whole family was overcome with grief. And on top of their sadness, they faced even more financial worries. They had less money than ever. Each week more and more unpaid bills piled up on the kitchen table.

Marian knew how desperate the situation was. One night she approached her mother with an idea she had been considering.

"Mama," she said, "I think I could make quite a lot of money if I worked full-time."

Mrs. Anderson frowned. "No," she said firmly. "I will not allow you to quit school. I never got the education I wanted. I won't let that happen to you."

Marian put her hand gently on her mother's shoulder. "But we need the money," she persisted. "And I wouldn't mind. Really I wouldn't."

"No," said Mrs. Anderson. "And that's final."

Marian sighed. In a way, she was relieved by her mother's decision, because she did not really want to quit school.

THE Andersons didn't know it, but at that very moment, members of their church were making plans to help them.

"For years our Marian has been singing for us," Mr. Robinson, the choirmaster, said to the church elders. "Now I think it's time we did something to help her."

The elders agreed. That Sunday they sent around a collection plate to help Marian and her family. Each member of the congregation gave whatever coins he or she could spare. In all, they collected $17.02.

"Here," said Mr. Robinson, when he presented the money to Marian. "We want you to use the money to buy a concert dress. That way you can sing at concerts in the neighborhood and all around the city. Maybe you will be able to earn some money."

Marian did not know what to say. She was overcome with gratitude. "Thank you," she whispered. "Thank you so much. I will always remember this."

Dressed in a white satin dress and new shoes, Marian began singing for local organizations. Mostly she sang gospel tunes and spirituals. Her audiences loved her.

Eventually she felt confident enough to charge for her performances. She gave most of her earnings to her mother to help with the family's expenses. She was proud to be able to help.

MARIAN continued singing in the Union Baptist Church choir. She was very serious about this commitment and never missed a single Sunday. Whenever the choir was practicing a new song, she learned the soprano and tenor parts as well as her own. Then if a soloist was absent, she could sing the song. She became an indispensable part of the church choir.

About this time, Marian decided that she could finally afford formal music training.

"At last!" she thought excitedly as she rode the bus to the music school. "At last I will learn a technique for singing. Now my songs will sound better than ever!"

At the music school a young woman sat behind a desk, answering questions and handing out application forms. When it was Marian's turn, the woman looked past her and spoke to the person behind her in line. Finally, there was no one else in line.

"What do you want?" the woman asked coldly.

Marian tried to ignore her tone. "I'd like an application form, please."

"We don't take colored people," the woman said pointedly, tossing her hair over her shoulder.

"But I have the money right here!" Marian said, tears rolling down her cheeks.

"I said we don't take colored!" the girl repeated angrily.

Marian was crushed. She lived in an integrated neighborhood and had never encountered anything like this before.

"Does this mean the end of my dreams? Does this mean I can't be a singer?" she asked her mother when she got home.

Mrs. Anderson thought for a moment, then replied in her slow, calm manner. "No, dear. There will be another way. If you want something badly enough, there will be a way to get it."

"That's just what I'll do," Marian resolved. "I'll keep looking until I find someone who will give me private lessons. Surely there must be someone in Philadelphia who is willing to teach me."

Marian's high school principal arranged an interview with a well-known voice teacher, Giuseppe Boghetti. Nervously, Marian entered the dimly lit room. Mr. Boghetti appeared exhausted and did not even rise from his armchair to greet her.

"I don't know why I agreed to this interview," he said gruffly. "I have too many students already. I don't want any more students. I'm only listening to you as a favor!"

Confused and even more nervous than before, Marian cleared her throat and began singing the song she had practiced.

Captivated, Mr. Boghetti leaned forward in his chair. Marian's voice seemed to brighten the room. When Marian finished singing, he said enthusiastically, "That was quite lovely. I have changed my mind. I will make room for you right away. After a few years of studying with me, you will be able to sing anywhere for anyone. One day you will sing for kings and queens, young lady!"

With Mr. Boghetti's help, Marian learned to discipline her voice to produce any note she wanted. She did special breathing exercises. She learned a whole new series of songs, including the works of classical masters such as Brahms and Schubert.

IN 1925 Marian entered a contest with three hundred other singers. The winner would be a guest soloist with the New York Philharmonic Symphony Orchestra. Marian won! Her confidence grew steadily, and by 1930, she felt ready to sing at the best concert halls in the country.

But once again, she found her path blocked.

"Sorry," people told her again and again. "Only white singers are allowed here."

Frustrated, Marian decided to take all her savings and travel to Europe.

"Maybe there people will care more about my talent than about my color," she thought.

She was not disappointed. In city after city, Marian Anderson captured the hearts of Europeans. In Stockholm, Sweden, newspapers declared that "Marian Fever" was sweeping the continent. Even the famous conductor Arturo Toscanini heaped praise on her. He told her, "A voice like yours is heard only once in a hundred years."

Buoyed by her success, Marian decided in 1935 to return to America.

"But why?" asked several of her European friends. "Why go back to a place where you are not appreciated?"

"I'm not just going back for myself," Marian explained. "There are other people to be considered — all my friends and neighbors who have believed in me for so many years. They didn't help me just to see me run away to Europe. I came here to achieve something, to become a serious musician. But I never doubted that I must return. For better or worse, I am an American."

WHEN she arrived back in America, Marian was relieved to see that some attitudes had changed. Her extraordinary performances in Europe opened many new doors for her. Suddenly it seemed that she was welcomed everywhere. When she gave a concert in New York, the tickets sold out almost overnight. And as her radiant voice filled the hall, the audience went wild. She was hailed as "a contralto of stunning range and volume." One paper even pronounced her "the world's greatest contralto."

Marian remembered her doubts and disappointments. She thought of her mother's words from so long ago.

"If you want something badly enough, there will be a way to get it."

Marian Anderson had wanted badly to make music her life. Through effort and perseverance, she was finally able to share her unique talent with the world.

AUDIE MURPHY

A HERO UNDER FIRE

More than anything, I want to be a soldier. But when I try to sign up, the recruiters all laugh at me. They say I'm too young and skinny and short. I just don't look like a soldier. But I know that I could do something to help the United States win the war, if they'd only give me the chance.

AUDIE Murphy looked around the ramshackle cabin near Greenville, Texas, where he lived with his eight brothers and sisters. Pretty soon, he knew, the cabin would be empty. Now that his mother had died, the children would be going to orphanages.

"Well, *I'm* not going to any orphanage," he thought obstinately. "One way or another, *I'm* going to join the military."

The next day Murphy walked timidly into a Marine recruiting station and asked to sign up.

"How old are you, son?" the sergeant asked.

"Seventeen," said Murphy.

"And how much do you weigh?"

"One hundred and ten pounds."

"Listen, son," said the man, "I appreciate your coming in. But the Marines need men — tough, rugged men. You're just a boy."

Murphy felt crushed, but he didn't give up. He tried to enlist with the paratroopers.

"I couldn't send a scrawny young thing like you up in an airplane," laughed the recruiting officer.

Embarrassed, Murphy walked dejectedly out of the office.

By the time he reached his home, Murphy's determination was stronger than ever. For the next two weeks he stuffed himself with cereal and biscuits. After putting on a few extra pounds, he walked, shoulders squared, into an Army recruiting station. In the gruffest voice he could muster, he announced that he wanted to enlist as a soldier. This time he was successful! And so, in the summer of 1942, Audie Murphy became a private in the United States Army.

Murphy had never been happier. He reported to basic training camp full of enthusiasm. But trouble awaited him. It began when he fainted on the drill field. Then fellow soldiers began calling him "Baby." One day his commanding officer took him out of infantry training.

"Son, I'd hate to send a pint-sized kid like you out on the battlefield," he said. "So I'm going to do you a favor. I'm going to transfer you to the school for cooks and bakers. Then maybe someday you can run a mess tent for soldiers."

Murphy stared at the officer in horror. He didn't want to be a cook or a baker. He wanted to be a soldier. He wanted to prove his worth on a battlefield. Most of all, he wanted to help the United States and other Allied forces defeat the Germans and the Axis powers in World War II.

"Lock me up, sir!" he replied. "Put me in the stockade. But please don't send me to cooks' school! I won't go! I just won't go!"

The officer looked at Murphy thoughtfully. "All right," he said at last. "I'll give you one more chance. But any more signs of weakness on the training field and you're finished. Understand?"

Murphy nodded. He made a silent pledge to himself to become the best soldier in his unit.

By July of 1943, Murphy had completed his basic training and was sent to Europe. He was stationed in Sicily, an island off the southern coast of Italy. Suddenly Murphy found himself in the middle of World War II. Day by day, a new sense of confidence emerged as he gained experience in battle and learned the rigors of combat.

ONE day he and his squad were scouting the beach, looking for enemy troops farther inland. Suddenly two enemy officers appeared, mounted on white horses. When the officers saw the Americans, they turned and galloped off to warn their comrades.

"Stop them!" cried the squad sergeant.

The American soldiers sprinted after the retreating horses. But Murphy knew that a chase would be useless. Instead of running, he dropped to his knee and raised his rifle. Taking quick aim, he fired two shots. The two officers tumbled off their horses.

"Good thinking, Murphy!" exclaimed the sergeant. "You react well under pressure! You did the right thing."

From that moment on, Murphy had the respect of every man in his regiment. He was soon promoted to corporal, then to sergeant, and finally to lieutenant. Time after time, in the midst of battle, Murphy showed a fearlessness that awed even experienced combat soldiers.

By the end of 1944, Murphy had won many honors for his actions on the battlefield. He had been awarded the Distinguished Service Cross, the Bronze Star, and the Silver Star. He had also received two Purple Hearts for wounds he suffered in action.

MURPHY'S most courageous act occurred in January 1945. His outfit, Company B, was in France, marching through snow and sleet toward the German border.

"We must capture these woods and the village of Holtzwihr," Lieutenant Leake told his men. "If we can take this area, we will clear the way for the Allies to move into Germany."

Murphy nodded grimly. He knew how important this campaign was. He also knew that hundreds of German troops and many enemy tanks held the region. It would not be an easy operation.

On January 25, the soldiers of Company B fought their way through the Riedwihr Woods. The forest blazed with enemy fire as the men fought the Germans from tree to tree.

Later that day, word came that Lieutenant Leake had been badly wounded. That meant that Murphy was the only officer left in the unit. At 3:00 A.M. on January 26, he assumed command of Company B.

A few hours later, Murphy received new orders. Company B was to march out of the forest toward Holtzwihr. The men were to dig trenches in the field and hold their position until reinforcements arrived.

Upon reaching their destination, Murphy ordered his men to dig foxholes. But beneath the thick layer of snow, the ground was frozen solid. They would not even have the protection of foxholes. Murphy felt the muscles in his neck tighten. Without backup tanks or heavy artillery to bombard the enemy, he feared that his company had little chance against the Germans.

When two American tank destroyers arrived at dawn, the whole company cheered and breathed a sigh of relief. At least they would have some support. Murphy also managed to reestablish radio contact with headquarters back in the forest. He was promised artillery support for the coming battle.

AT about two o'clock in the afternoon, Murphy saw six German tanks advancing toward Company B. Behind the tanks marched more than 200 German soldiers, all dressed in white snowcapes. As Murphy took in this chilling sight, his knees felt weak. Armed only with a map, a pair of binoculars, a field telephone, and his carbine, he resolved to do his best.

The German tanks soon hit one of the American tank destroyers, leaving it smoking. The other American tank destroyer slid off the icy road and was helplessly stuck in a ditch.

Without the protection of the tank destroyers, Murphy knew his men didn't have a chance of holding their position.

"Get back to the woods!" he yelled to them.

The men started retreating. One looked back and called out to Murphy, "Hey, Lieutenant, aren't you coming?"

"Don't worry about me!" Murphy called. "Just get going!"

The men disappeared behind the trees. Alone on the open battlefield, Murphy picked up his field telephone and ran over to the burning tank destroyer. He crawled on top and peered over the turret. He could see the Germans advancing steadily toward him.

He began giving orders to the artillery men deep in the woods, using his field telephone to direct their aim.

"Correct your fire," he said to them. "Aim 100 yards in front of me."

With shells crashing closer and closer, Murphy grabbed the mounted machine gun and began shooting at the Germans. Lying flat on top of the smoking tank destroyer, he knew he could be blown apart at any moment. Artillery fire rained down around him. And still waves of Germans kept coming closer. Again Murphy used his field telephone to direct the artillery.

"Aim 20 yards in front of the tank I'm lying on," he commanded.

"Lieutenant Murphy, how close is the enemy to you?" an alarmed voice from headquarters asked.

"Hold the phone, I'll let you talk to one of them," Murphy quipped.

For the next hour, the Germans used every weapon they had to try and dislodge Murphy. Surrounded on three sides by German fire, Murphy was numb with fear. But he knew that he was doing the right thing. By staying on top of the destroyed tank, he could tell the American artillery where to fire. And he could slow down the enemy's advance by using the machine gun.

UST when it looked as if the enemy soldiers were so close they would surely take Murphy, the German tanks and troops stopped, turned around, and marched back to the village. Apparently, their commanders were discouraged by the high number of casualties.

When the battle was finally over, Murphy trembled with relief. His body was covered with bloody cuts from flying shrapnel. And his leg wounds from the previous day were throbbing. But, miraculously, he was alive!

Later, Murphy was asked why he sent his men back to the woods and faced the enemy alone.

"I saw no reason for any more men to be killed when one man could do the job," he replied.

Audie Murphy's courage and concern for others were proven in battle after battle. By the time he returned home to Texas, he was the most decorated American soldier in all of World War II.

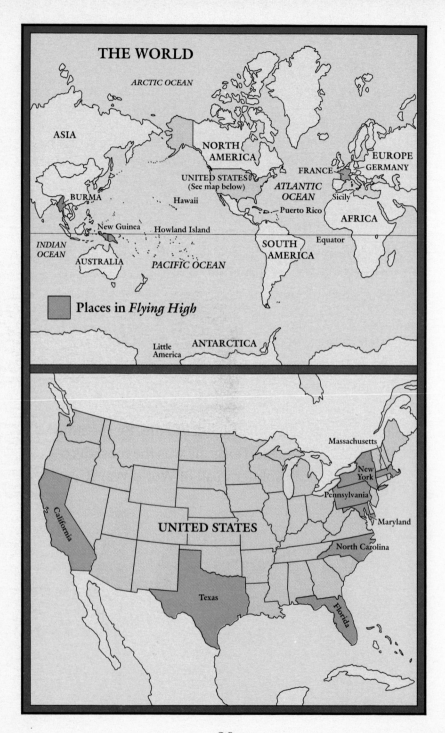

THE WORLD

ARCTIC OCEAN

ASIA

NORTH
AMERICA

EUROPE

GERMANY

FRANCE

UNITED STATES
(See map below)

ATLANTIC
OCEAN

Sicily

BURMA

Hawaii

Puerto Rico

AFRICA

New Guinea

Howland Island

Equator

INDIAN
OCEAN

SOUTH
AMERICA

AUSTRALIA

PACIFIC OCEAN

Places in *Flying High*

Little
America

ANTARCTICA

Massachusetts

New
York

Pennsylvania

Maryland

California

UNITED STATES

North Carolina

Texas

Florida